Surviving Me

Journeys Through Managing Anxiety and Stress and Finding Spiritual Peace

Gail Fripp

Copyright ©2018 by Gail Fripp

All rights reserved. No portion of this book may be reproduced in any form or by any electronic or mechanical means including photocopying, recording, and information storage and retrieval systems – except in the case of brief quotations embodied in critical articles or reviews – without permission in writing from the publisher.

DISCLAIMER: This book is not medical advice. It is for informational purposes only. Apart from a few facts, these are personal accounts of overcoming or dealing with anxiety and stress. Please seek medical advice from a professional when necessary.

Printed in the United States of America

Publisher: 3R Inspired Media

ISBN-13: 978-1-7322581-0-5

ISBN-10: 1732258104

Editing/Proofreading: Kareem Ali, Najee Ali, Lettia Shaw

GailFripp.com

Dedication

This book is dedicated to all the women suffering from anxiety and stress. It is also dedicated to those desiring a stronger spiritual connection but are struggling with it. I want to thank my family for the support they have given me over the years and for putting up with my ascension to becoming a healthier, stronger woman. There aren't enough words to describe how much I love you all. I am so very grateful that Allah blessed me with your beautiful souls. To my friends who have supported me and pushed me and have given me strength when I doubted mine - you are true treasures and I honor you. What you gave me I will do my best to give back to you. To the ladies who gave their stories for inclusion in this book, I am so grateful for your gifts. You will help so many with your transparency. You have no idea how many you will touch. Thank you is not enough.

Without God, I am nothing.

"...Our Lord, grant us from Yourself mercy and prepare for us from our affair right guidance."

Quran 18:10

"No weapon formed against you shall prosper..."

Isaiah 54:17

Table of Contents

Introduction	7
From Anxiety to Awareness	10
Recognizing Anxiety and Stress	14
How Your Anxiety and Stress Affects Others	21
Uncomfortable Guidance	25
Too Old to Change	28
Help Yourself, Even in Small Ways	31
Words Are Powerful	36
Spirituality and Spiritual Imbalance	39
The Guiding Heart	49
Personal Stories and Observations	55
Reflections	89
Conclusion	97
Resources	98
About the Author	99

Introduction

I have been given a test in life. I have been given the opportunity to positively affect others by learning information and passing it along so that they may benefit. It feels heavy on my chest – not a heaviness of negativity and doom, but a heaviness of responsibility, love, and understanding. It energizes me and gives me life. It reminds me of why I am here and guides me towards what is important. It's not necessarily an easy test though. I experience feelings of doubt about my choices and wonder if I'm doing enough. It's fairly normal to feel this way. I just want to do the best I can with whatever I have available. Though it is challenging, I welcome the challenge and feel that I am blessed to have it.

It is my hope that when you read this book, you feel a connection to it. I pray that it is able to give you a sense of belonging to a family larger than you thought possible. It is my greatest desire that it helps you look at your situation with a new and positive perspective and gives you new life. You can make changes to your life starting today that can be beneficial to you and your loved ones now and in the future. After you read it, pass it along to another who may benefit or better yet, get them their own copy. I'm cheering for you. Thank you for reading this. May you be richly rewarded for taking steps to help yourself or someone you love.

Quick Lesson

Something I have noticed is that when I truly desire change, and I can feel this desire to change in my heart and in my whole body, then help starts to arrive in various forms. I begin to see messages in my social media feed that supports me. I begin to receive messages from others out of the blue that are encouragements to me. I begin to see stories that are similar to what I am trying to achieve. It is truly amazing when it happens, and you may not always be ready when it arrives. The point is, it doesn't always have to be a physical person standing next to you supporting you and guiding you. Help comes from unexpected places and it is up to you to recognize these things when you are ready.

Chapter 1

From Anxiety to Awareness

I have lost myself in a story that I wrote all by myself. I was the main character. I was the catalyst. I was the antagonist, the bully, and the hero. The setting was my entire life. It never changed. I came and went as I pleased and was late for my own arrival. The magnificent thing about this story is that it is still being written.

Throughout my journey with anxiety, I have been up and down and somewhere in the middle. I have been trying to figure out if I could muster up the strength to rise again after I fell. There were days when I attempted to take a deep breath in and it seemed that I could not inhale enough to satisfy my needs. I do have asthma, but that was not it. It was because I was suffocating myself with this sickness and fear of the unknown. It was almost as if I felt that if I got a full breath, then I had somehow relaxed too much, and that was unacceptable. My life's mission seemed to be to control everything I touched. If I couldn't control it, or understand it, or guide it instantly, I had to worry about it until I figured out how to do just that. I could not rest until everything was comfortable for me and the space that I was in – until everything aligned precisely in the manner that I had pictured in my most organized and logical mind.

There was only one problem...ok...there were many problems. Despite all my best intentions to control the world, I was forgetting some things. Where was my focus in prayer? Where was the support for me? Where was my ability to ask for help when I needed it most? Why did I feel the need to handle almost everything alone? Where or how did I learn that? How could I return to a healthy, balanced spiritual and personal life after living and submitting to such a consistently unbalanced one?

I wasn't even going to write this book. I didn't think it was important enough to put out into the world and have any effect at all. But what I noticed was that when I began to speak and when I began to tell the story of my struggles and how I overcame some of my huge issues, others began to react. People began to open up to me and tell me about their own struggles and their own battles. They began to tell me the devastation that had occurred because of their anxiety and stress. It was almost like having this secret little family that was just waiting for one member to speak so that the rest could also speak. It is quite amazing to have such a connection to others regarding something that can be so overwhelming. We are kindred spirits who huddle around a fire that burns us daily. Yet we find comfort in one another. We know what the other is going through, and we respect our battles.

What was also stressed to me by them was that I should definitely write a book or begin speaking about this problem. They began to encourage me and let me know that I was not alone - that there are so many people who suffer from this and that someone must speak out for those who can't. Because of that, it was no longer whether I wanted to do something or whether it was possible for me to do something. The questions became when I was going to do it, on what scale would I do it, and would it be possible for me to help even one person through this. I began to feel a sense of great responsibility.

If I was able to overcome something or if I had tools to help someone, then how could I keep going without doing so? Was I given a gift for a reason? I had to find out. I had to push the limits that I did not realize could be pushed. No matter what, through all the fear, through all of the anxiety, I had to push forward in order to help others step forward even once. This was my trial. This was my destiny.

~ **Destiny called. I answered.** ~

"I've learned that you shouldn't go through life with a catcher's mitt on both hands; you need to be able to throw something back." Maya Angelou

Chapter 2

Recognizing Anxiety and Stress

When anxiety and stress make themselves known, there is a weight that sits on you that feels like it never wants to leave. It holds you back from just about everything you could imagine. Places you want to go seem too far away to reach. Things you want to do no longer seem fun because you can't relax. Entertaining this pair is no way to live. They can destroy your friendships, your business, and even your family relationships and marriage.

I used to avoid going places for fear of someone I might see - for fear that I would not be able to handle the situation that I was walking into. Then I realized, I had so much that I wanted to do and so much that I wanted to give that this behavior was not an option for me any longer. I had to go out no matter the fear. I had to face it head-on if I was to achieve my greatest dreams. I had to understand what a normal level of hesitation for me was and what was beyond normal. If I didn't do this, every situation would become one that was unbearable and unmanageable. I recognized the need for change and I began to move. Because of that decision, I am much happier today. I want that for you as well.

Quick Lesson

One of the most important lessons that I have learned throughout my life, is that I must walk in fear and anxiety. If I give up along the way, my path to success ends there. I have always been active in sports and social activities throughout my life, but the majority of the time, I have always felt butterflies in the stomach, and the urge to throw up, or something along those lines. Ultimately, if I wanted what I wanted, I was going to have to walk forward no matter what. I have accomplished many things, and I have managed to walk even taller in the midst of my anxiety and my fears. This is a skill that must continually be addressed and strengthened. As long as I move forward, I am progressing, and I will succeed. Success is in my eyes not in the eyes of another. Only I know what hurdles I have crossed and what I have overcome.

Understanding What's Normal and What May Need Attention

We live in a lifetime where the media and even friends and family are telling us what normal reactions are to various life challenges. We are told how to react "properly" when being stopped by police, when being disrespected by others, and when losing our jobs without warning while having bills to pay. We are told how long is acceptable to stay in a struggling, yet non-abusive relationship, how to lose weight quickly, and the list goes on. But the problem with that is, none of us are the same so we will not have the same reaction.

We are all born with our own unique set of tools to deal with challenges. We all have unique ways of accepting, responding to, and even solving our problems. We all have our own levels of tolerance and patience. We are all different by design.

So, what is our "normal" reaction when dealing with anxiety and stress? What are healthy ways to overcome our obstacles? Those are the things that we need to be looking at. When we reveal this, we will be well on our way to gaining the balance that we need within our lives. The first step that needs to be taken to facilitate finding solutions is accepting the fact that we need changes – not just knowing it, but accepting it. We must also be willing to make those changes once they are revealed to us. Nothing happens without action.

Facts - AADA
Let's take a look at some facts from T*he Anxiety and Depression Association of America* (ADAA). I don't want to give too many because I want this book to be a true

connection between me, you, and so many others in similar situations.

The ADAA offers an enormous amount of information. It categorizes anxiety as a mental illness. The term mental illness is one that has a stigma attached to it. I don't know of anyone who wants to be labeled as being in this state. Because of this, people find that they try to work through their anxiety and stress and claim that it is just how they are. They are reluctant to get professional help. For some, this is a huge mistake. There is no working through or getting beyond your problem if it has consumed your entire life. You should consider seeking help.

While there are always exceptions when viewing statistics, this is meant to give you an idea of the common signs and prevalence of anxiety.

- Anxiety disorders are highly treatable, yet only about one-third of those suffering receive treatment.[1]

- Anxiety disorders are the most common mental illness in the U.S., affecting 40 million adults in the United States age 18 and older, or 18% of the population. (Source: National Institute of Mental Health)[2]

---

[1] Anxiety and Depression Association of America. https://www.adaa.org/about-adaa/press-room/facts-statistics
[2] ibid

- Anxiety disorders develop from a complex set of risk factors, including genetics, brain chemistry, personality, and life events.[3]

Generalized Anxiety Disorder (GAD)[4]

- Affects 6.8 million adults or 3.1 percent of the U.S. population.

- Characterized by persistent and excessive worry about a number of different things.

- Individuals with GAD find it difficult to control their worry. They may worry more than seems warranted about actual events or may expect the worst even when there is no apparent reason for concern.

- Some people can have difficulty carrying out the simplest daily activities when their anxiety is severe.

  GAD is diagnosed in adults when they experience at least three of the symptoms below on more days than not for at least six months; only one symptom is required in children.[5]

---

[3] ibid
[4] Anxiety and Depression Association of America.
 https://www.adaa.org/understanding-anxiety/generalized-anxiety-disorder-gad
[5] Anxiety and Depression Association of America.https://www.adaa.org/understanding-anxiety/generalized-anxiety-disorder-gad/symptoms

Symptoms of GAD include the following:

- restlessness or feeling keyed up or on edge
- being easily fatigued
- difficulty concentrating or mind going blank
- irritability
- muscle tension
- sleep disturbance (difficulty falling or staying asleep, or restless, unsatisfying sleep)

The website goes on to show the links between anxiety and depression and how they mimic one another. What I have stated in this book isn't even half of what is available, but even this tiny bit gives an idea of how great the issue of anxiety is.

These facts are not a diagnosis of your state. If you feel that you cannot handle your daily life and have been struggling for a long period of time, you may need to seek more help – help that is beyond just talking to friends or engaging in relaxation techniques or prayer. Give yourself a chance to live a better life.

Chapter 3

How Your Anxiety and Stress Affects Others

Let's just start by saying that when you are an anxiety sufferer, ignoring the fact until later or failing to deal with how it manifests is not fixing it. It filters down to those around you, especially your children, spouse, and close family and friends. When anxiety and stress touch your children, it changes them. That happy, sweet, little person that you once knew becomes someone who barely wants to leave the home. Sometimes they tremble when asked questions. They get angry when things don't go their way or when it seems as if they cannot figure out a problem.

Have you ever watched the body language and facial expression of a child being degraded by an adult who is supposed to care about them? Have you witnessed their developing confidence slowly wither away as they struggle to please someone who won't acknowledge their achievements? I hope I have struck a nerve with you and made you pay attention. In these sad situations, the child loses unless the adult takes responsibility for his or her own anxious behavior. It cannot be ignored. It may come blasting to the surface later in the form of irritability, screaming, or worse!

Right now, at this very moment, you are making choices that will ultimately affect all you touch. Do you think that you are hiding it? Children and others around you are very observant. They internalize your feelings whether you know it or not. They may even begin to feel a sense of responsibility to compensate in areas that you have shown anxiety or stress over. For instance, your little one consistently sees you screaming or being unsettled because a toy is left out. In response, when she sees you coming, she may immediately run to pick it up and make a point to tell you that it was not laying out in the open.

There is a noticeable difference between a child who wants to be helpful and a child who is reacting to your stress and anxiety. You may not notice it right away, but others around you will notice it and may even bring it to your attention. Once that happens, the cycle of anxiety in your child may have already begun. You will have to work hard to reverse it or, at the very least, give them the tools to help them cope with their feelings better. Remember, you may not be the cause of their anxiety, but you may be an enabler based on your own actions.

In the case of your husband, your constant state of stress can damage the communication between you two, which may filter down into your intimate life. What I have learned personally and through other women and men is that when a man is not sure how to help you, he may pull back. He sees a situation that he cannot remedy within his own household, though he's trying so hard, and it's not even completely on him to fix! You have given him very little room to be there for you if you are not choosing to help yourself. Adding a caveat, I am assuming that your husband is not the main cause of your stress in the first place and he is not the one allowing it to continue. As always, when your relationship is extremely strained, you may need a professional to help you both work through it. You may need that anyway in the case of anxiety. It is just that powerful of an issue.

So, you see how this works? When you attempt to hide your challenges and save them to be worked on later, assuming you can gamble with your time, you could be affecting many people around you. What about them? Even after you have dealt with your issues, the negative effects on others will remain. They will need help to get beyond their experiences. You must be prepared to put in the work.

Some friends and family may not be able to forgive you for the way you made them feel whether intentional or not. Prepare to accept that as well while still trying to maintain your progress and repair your relationships with them.

Chapter 4

Uncomfortable Guidance

Let's talk about being uncomfortable for a moment. I have achieved many things, but often times I was uncomfortable striving for that success. I worried about people focusing on me, and I worried about disappointing myself. Believe it or not, I also worried about succeeding. Success means responsibility and setting higher goals. That can be scary! Obviously, it never completely stopped me. It was, however, extremely annoying to keep experiencing these feelings over and over again.

Sometimes, uncomfortable feelings mean that you should not do a task. I am a firm believer that when you have feelings that are preventing you from something, you should pay attention. I believe that we are guided, and we miss cues when they are given to us. Our job is to decipher whether those feelings are preventing us from doing something bad, or whether it is our minds preventing us from achieving something good. I would venture to say that many of us often hold our own selves back when we are being guided towards greatness. It is as if we can't believe that something good would actually be sent our way, especially not in the form of Supreme guidance. I mean, who are we to be led towards something positive and great?

Sometimes we grow frustrated about being alone during uncomfortable times. It may actually be a sign helping us to focus and pay more attention to the task at hand. Sometimes it is not meant for us to have several people or even one person next to us to guide us to the next step. Sometimes we are meant to stand on our own two feet and take the next step alone. Is it uncomfortable? Yes. Is there an alternative? Yes. The alternative is for you to stand still in all of your uncomfortable feelings and stay exactly where you are. I don't believe that is your goal. You cannot let a lack of support from others stop you achieving your dreams. Take one small step today and another step tomorrow, but never stop.

Chapter 5

Too Old to Change?

Let's address age for a moment. When did you come up with this idea that getting older meant no more time to change? Who told you that because you had been set in your ways for so long, you would never be able to do anything differently than how you do it now? Whoever said that is out of touch with the strength that is deep within you. If you woke up this morning, and you are still breathing and able, then you have a chance to change your life.

I have listened to older people for so long saying that this is just how it is. They state that there is no more time for them to do anything different. So, they sit and wallow in the circumstances that they have been given. They react to stresses the same way they always have. They see no light and no way out. Even if they wanted to change, they don't believe that putting in the effort is worth it. So, for these people, they have given up their dreams of ever becoming the better versions of themselves that they have desired for so long. They have become comfortable in their own misery or lack of determination.

To me, this is unacceptable behavior. There is no time in life that you are unable to at least attempt to reach your dreams, aside from times of poor health or other challenges. As long as you have breath in your body, you can strive to create the life that you want. To sit back and accept defeat is not a solution.

I have family members who have gone through so much tragedy, including the death of a spouse or child, serious illness, and more. Guess what? They never quit! They were challenged beyond all belief. Some days they felt that it would never get any better. They had to work harder than maybe they had ever worked in their lives. I am not only speaking about those who are in their twenties or thirties. I am speaking of those well beyond those years. They fought hard to get back to a point where they could just breathe regularly again, and they didn't stop there. Knowingly and unknowingly, they breathed life into those around them. They became benchmarks for where others wished that they could be. They were role models for those going through rough times but wanting to get through them. They held on even in their older age, and those still with us continue to hold on to this day.

There is no timer on you reaching a goal other than your own determination. There is no comparing it to what others have reached. This is about you and your desire to be a better you. This is about you overcoming great challenges that have left you feeling beaten and defeated. This is about the resurrection of your own true self and it is powered by your desires to move forward. Never tell yourself or let others tell you that age is a barrier for you. It is a lie. I have seen it over and over again. I'm sure if you look around you, you will see examples of people who have fought hard just to see the next day. Never give up. Age is truly nothing but a number.

Chapter 6

Help Yourself, Even in Small Ways

We sometimes believe that in order to make the biggest impact on our lives we have to make a huge leap forward. Who told you that? If you have no pressing need to move at light speed to your next threshold of success, then take smaller steps that give you the confidence and the momentum to want to keep going! The most consistently done actions, whether for religious purposes, financial purposes, or personal goals, are the ones that stay with you the longest. They become second nature if done often enough and pave the way for you to reach your goals almost on autopilot.

I was reading an article about forming habits. It stated that there is a theory that it takes 21 days to do so. This idea came from a plastic surgeon in the 1950s named Maxwell Maltz[6]. Maltz actually stated that it takes a MINIMUM of 21 days to form a new habit or change your mindset. It was others who made 21 days concrete. The point is, if you are consistent and have a desire to make the change, you will eventually get there. You don't have to rush.

Let me give you an example. The stress of having to share your child with your ex-husband or wife consistently gives you stomach pain and headaches. You feel tense and are ready to argue at the drop of a dime. Question: Aren't you

---

[6] Clear, James. "How Long Does It Actually Take To Form A New Habit (Backed by Science)" *Huffington Post,* 04/10/2014 Updated 06/10/2014, www.huffingtonpost.com/james-clear/forming-new-habits_b_5104807.html.

tired of feeling that way? Aren't you tired of defending yourself when there may be nothing to defend in the first place? Don't confuse my words and think that I am talking about cases where there has been extreme violence (or any violence for that matter) and tension is warranted. I am referring to cases where having extreme stress is well within your ability to change – cases where you are refusing to move past a situation that did not work in your favor and you are dragging it out for as long as you are able. In these cases, you know that it is unhealthy, yet you refuse to let it go.

When you DECIDE that you want relief from making yourself sick week after week or day after day, you will begin to move forward. You can start by choosing to accept what your ex-spouse is doing that is good and giving them room to make mistakes. After all, you are not perfect in your actions or words either. You can refuse to react in the same manner that you normally do and that is small step number 1 (or HUGE step number 1) that can be consistently done until it becomes natural to you. You are now forming a new habit that benefits you and probably those surrounding you. You have now begun to move forward.

If You Want Better, Change is a Must

Many times, I have listened to the words of others complaining of all that was wrong in their lives and all that was done to them. I have watched them drown in their own misery with no end in sight. It is such a sad sight to see and I don't wish this pain on anyone. I just wanted to go to them, grab and shake them, and let them know that they must put in the effort to change their own circumstances. One of those people that I wanted to shake was me!

There have been times in my life where I was unable to get past something that was said or done to me, or a choice that I made. I allowed the incident to replay in my mind almost continuously. It was devastating to feel the effects of my thoughts on my body and on those surrounding me. It felt as if I was watching from outside of myself - like I was no longer me and was living inside of a movie that never ended. I didn't fully accept the responsibility I had for making my own choices to move beyond this barrier. Situations like this in anyone's life can be confusing, frustrating, and definitely overwhelming.

I felt deep within my soul that it truly was me driving this negative attitude that I had. I knew that it was not healthy or beneficial to be in that state of mind. However, acknowledging that openly meant that I would have to take action. That was the scary part. Taking action to change your life can mean several things, including possible failure at what you are trying to achieve. What I had to understand was that even if I failed the first time, I at least made the effort to keep going. I had to believe that no matter what was coming, I would get the best result in the end. I had to keep moving even with anxiety and fear.

Today I realize that even though deciding to actively make changes was scary, it was actually quite refreshing. It felt like a weight was lifted off my shoulders. I knew what I had to do, and the only thing left was to begin the process of getting back to the true me. That was one of the best days of my life. My whole world looked different from that point on. Imagine what it would look like if you did the same?

Quick Lesson

You must desire to change first, then the deeper mental and physical action begins. Can you choose to accept that you made mistakes in the past? You do know we all make mistakes. It is just part of who we are as humans. If you cannot forgive yourself for a mistake that you made, you will never be able to find that serenity within yourself. Each time you think you are moving forward, the memory of your mistake will pop up and you will slide back into old thoughts of self-doubt, anger, and more stress. You will consistently be living in an unsustainable, fake world of happiness that only leads you into wondering who you truly are.

Chapter 7

Words Are Powerful

One of the phrases that I have heard many times throughout my adult life from women is this: "I feel defeated." I don't know about you, but when I hear this phrase, it immediately evokes a feeling of dread, doom, despair, and a feeling that the one who utters it will never rise. Is this the way you feel? Do you feel that you will never get out of this situation, or that you will never be blessed with anything better than what you have?

It is a rhetorical question for some of you. For others, I will assume that you have never thought of it in this way. You may have never truly listened to yourself as you spoke those words. It has just become a phrase you use when you are down and have experienced a tremendous amount of stress. I would gather that you never thought of the weight that you added to your shoulders when those words fell from your mouth like a ton of bricks reinforced with steel pipes and coated in lead.

Words are extremely powerful and can push you over the edge or can hold you down for long periods of time. This phrase, "I feel defeated", is one that should live in a black hole never to see light again. When allowed to roll off your tongue, you have immediately placed a barrier in your path. You must recognize that this state of mind is not healthy. Then, you must work hard to overcome it. Is this easy to do? Am I judging you based on your circumstances? No, it is not easy and no I am not judging you. I am cheering for your success and I recognize where you are in your life.

I understand the meaning of feeling defeat, but I cannot let you stay in that state of mind. My job is to help you acknowledge the weight of these words, so that you are better able to find what you seek personally, financially, and spiritually. Those words are dream killers and life killers. You must understand this. They dictate your future if you do not change your mindset.

Chapter 8

Spirituality & Spiritual Imbalance

Spirituality

What is spirituality anyway? I looked it up, asked real people, and read articles and books surrounding "spiritual" concepts. What I found is that the definition varies according to who you are speaking to and what you are reading. Because of that, I am going to provide the dictionary definitions of religion and spirituality and then lead with my own interpretation and how it supports my life to this day.

According to Merriam-Webster dictionary, religion[7] is:

(1) the service and worship of God or the supernatural

(2) commitment or devotion to religious faith or observance

(3) a personal set or institutionalized system of religious attitudes, beliefs, and practices

The definition of spiritual[8] is:

(1) of, relating to, consisting of, or affecting the spirit: incorporeal spiritual needs

(2) concerned with religious values

(3) related or joined in spirit - our spiritual home - his spiritual heir

---

[7] "Religion." *Merriam-Webster.com.* Merriam-Webster, n.d. Web. 12 Mar. 2018.
[8] "Spiritual." *Merriam-Webster.com.* Merriam-Webster, n.d. Web. 13 Mar. 2018.

(4) of or relating to supernatural beings or phenomena

As you can see, these definitions are very basic. Religion is service, devotion, and an institutionalized system of beliefs. Spirituality has a greater freedom of interpretation but still has a connection to religion. This is probably why it is so appealing to those desiring a relationship with something greater than themselves. You don't have to call it religion, but you can still gain a sense of peace when engaged in it.

In my eyes, spirituality is a component of religion and they both must work together for your greatest benefit. It is taking that religious foundation, internalizing it, and making that deeper connection to God. That is what holds you together every single day. It is one of the most important things that one could attain in life.

Spirituality is that essence that gives you peace throughout the day. It's that presence that helps you feel grounded when it seems that your mind is so scattered that you can't see clearly. It is the force that you feel is keeping you in check. That is why you hear people state that they are spiritual but not religious; however, if the two concepts were truly taught as one unit that uplifted your soul with guidance AND connection to that Great Life Force, then there would be no need to distinguish between the two.

Within the last few years, I have realized the great importance of spirituality. My husband and my sons had begun the journey to strengthen their own before I jumped all in. They were listening to lectures, reading books, consulting one another, and talking about what they had learned and the strides they had made. That was the sense of peace that I wanted. So I began to look at spirituality in another light.

I looked at how it differed from the practice of religion, how the two were connected, and how I could use them to better myself. It was one of the best journeys that I could have ever started. Though I have a long way to go on this journey, I have learned to keep my mind open to various ideas. These ideas could be the difference between me feeling peace, and me not knowing where my next journey will take me or how I will handle it.

Talking to My Children About Maintaining Spirituality

I often talk to my children about maintaining a spiritual connection to their Creator. It seems like another "parent talk", but truly it is something they should take to heart. They never know when they're going to need this connection, which is why it is so important.

Some days there is nothing left except your lifeline to God - those days where you are emotionally and physically beat down. You must hold on to that spiritual rope with everything that you have. What is hard to see is when your child finally realizes what this mean. They reach a crossroads in their life and have no idea where to go. It's hard to see, but when they come to you and ask you how to handle the situation, it makes you feel as if you did a good job raising them.

Spirituality is so underrated. If I cannot connect to my Creator, I don't have a leg to stand on. I have never learned a lesson as intensely as I have learned this one within these last few years. I have struggled with so many things and I have asked so many questions of myself and of God. All of those questions began to be answered when I gave in and I allowed God to take over. That is when I realized how important spirituality is in the connection to God. There is nothing else like it and I would not give it up for anything.

Some have never had this experience in their entire lives. I feel sorry for those people, because they will never know the peace that is felt once that weight of having to support the world is released. It is a rebirth of self. Removing that weight can feel strange because it has been held onto for so long; however, once you get rid of it, you will understand how precious that feeling is. You will learn to embrace it and never release it. When you begin to feel that you are straying from that path of peace, you will correct yourself with your connection to God.

Spiritual Imbalance

Keeping your spiritual balance can be a bit of a task. When you have it, you feel its ability to keep your mind focused and at peace. When you don't have it, you may not know what's wrong, but you know you don't feel settled.

You Feel Distant and Tired

So how do you know that you may have a spiritual imbalance? One way you can tell is if you begin to feel distant from everyone and tired. It is almost as if you are there, but you are watching from outside of your body. It can feel as if there is a clear barrier around you that no one can penetrate. You may not even know that it is there right away, but those who encounter you clearly feel it.

When you go throughout your day, you are not connecting to anyone or anything in particular. You are just surviving each day wondering when it will be over. Because you are not connecting with others right now, you feel like an outsider. You feel as if no one understands where you are coming from and it drains you constantly. Getting out of the bed to greet each day becomes a major chore and nothing appears that it will give you relief from this feeling. You are at a standoff with your own mind and body; nobody is going to win this battle.

If you are spiritually in tune with your Creator and the world around you, you will find that you are being given relief at many turns. What you are being shown may not be complete relief; however, you are being guided in a direction that will lead you to the beginning of personal peace.

You Can't Pray or Struggle to Pray

How else can you tell you are lacking spiritual balance? One of the hardest situations that has ever occurred in my life was that I was struggling to pray. This was before I was even Muslim. I'm not talking about formal prayers. I'm saying I was struggling to ask for anything at all – EVER! It was one of the most challenging internal battles that I felt I had no control over. I just kept feeling as if prayer was not available for me. I believed that others were more deserving of receiving relief for their issues because mine were "not that bad." With that thinking, I actually put myself in a worse position than I was originally in. I had taken away my ability to receive the blessings from the only One who was able to offer them. I had moved myself further away from receiving the spiritual balance that I so desired.

It is amazing how outside forces and internal negativity can guide you towards staying in a place of suffering and detriment - sometimes for a lifetime. You want out of this mindset, but you are unable to encourage yourself to do so. The solutions are right in front of your face, but they appear to be millions of miles away. I find it quite fascinating actually. The messages that we give ourselves are so powerful. We still strongly believe the negativity, but we don't consider the fact that positive thoughts with the same intensity can bring great success in life. We sabotage our own lives, yet we somehow blame it on the acts of others. This is incredible.

Prayer gives us relief. Prayer forces us to consider a power greater than our own mind. Prayer is the soft pillow to lay your head on and the warm blanket that gives you security at night. Prayer is the strength that our muscles use to hold us up when all we want to do is fall. Prayer is that falling star you see that leaves you amazed at the wonders and the beauty of the night and the light you see when you close your eyes and are laying in a pitch-black room. Prayer is the tingling you feel when you have given up all hope and then something wonderful happens. Prayer is a companion of spiritual balance and is never just an option. It is an integral part of the total package.

So, the next time you feel that you cannot pray or that you are struggling to pray, know that this is only a test for you. Prayer is like a lifeline - like an umbilical cord that connects you to life. Never believe it to be insignificant. It may be the only thing keeping you from giving life up completely. The struggle you go through is a testament to the strength that you have forgotten you have or the strength that you have not yet discovered. Keep fighting. I believe you can make it through. I did, and I stand prepared to do battle with my negative mind over and over again.

You Can't Discuss Your Religion Because of Doubt

Another way you can tell if your spiritual balance is lacking is when you hesitate about spreading your religion. An imbalance has a way of creating doubt in your mind. It can make you believe that you are an impostor or a hypocrite – saying you believe in God and His words but failing to move closer or feel closer to Him. What you must realize is that not you, nor anyone else, is perfect in their practice of religion.

We all make mistakes and none of us are all-knowing. We have struggles and we have doubts. Those troubles and doubts should not prevent us from at least discussing spirituality or our purpose in this life. Sometimes, these are the conversations that take us to a higher state of belief. The doubts that we have may be the doubts that others also have. By sharing them with someone you trust, you will be strengthening yourself and hopefully clarifying areas that you were struggling with.

So, when you believe that you are unable to share your religion or your spiritual knowledge because you doubt your own belief in such knowledge, then only pass along those things that you are solid on and research the things that you feel confusion about. Don't give up everything based on your weakness in one area. You are able to teach even by your actions. Never forget that. We learn from one another constantly and you are part of that learning circle. Increase your knowledge and pass along what you know. Someone is always listening, watching, and learning from you and you from them.

Chapter 9

The Guiding Heart

The Heart

Throughout my journey with anxiety and stress, I have learned to listen to the tugging of my heart. When it is uneasy, I listen. When it aches, I listen. When it loves, I listen. When it warns, I listen. Some call it intuition. I agree, but I think it's much more than that if you pay attention. The heart is this incredible muscle that moves involuntarily. It pumps whether you tell it to or not. It has no regard for whether you are comfortable with the information that it is sending. It serves to sustain you and guide you. This makes it an incredibly intuitive machine – a machine that runs on spiritual vibrations and not any input from us. It is efficient. It is accurate. It is the best guide that we have in our physical lives to tell us when there is danger, where there is love, and when we need to slow down a bit. To ignore it could be fatal for you.

Since I have learned the power of the heart, I have honed in on its ability to strengthen me in my daily life. I am now more open to it giving me clues into how I should live my life. I trust it and use it as one of my closest advisors. It doesn't fail me when I use this approach.

Have you ever fought and fought yourself to make a decision that you knew was probably the best for you? You felt it throughout your entire body, yet you still refused to make the choice. You cried. You screamed. Your anxiety and stress were through the roof. You did everything you could to ignore yourself and those around you who were showing you the better choice. When you stopped fighting what you were feeling and began to listen to your heart's guidance, it was probably only then that positive things began to happen for you. You were shown the path. When you stopped and were quiet, you opened yourself up to be led by a spiritual presence - by God.

When this happened for me, it was one of the most liberating feelings I had ever felt. I wondered why I had not succumbed to this acceptance before. Maybe stubbornness, or arrogance, or something else that did not want me to progress in my life for one reason or another. I still have my days where I hesitate briefly, but for the most part those days are over. I give up. I am open to being led by my heart and my spirit. I am open to being loved by someone or something I cannot see yet has my best interest in mind. I am open to releasing myself to accept powers beyond what I can conceive. It creates a whole new realm of possibilities for me and for my family.

When I am at my best, I have the ability to help guide my family towards their best. I can teach them what I know. It is now my responsibility to share the gem that I have found and let them find their own path to spiritual peace and life success.

Spirituality and the Broken Heart

Let me ask you this, when one says that they have a broken heart, is it truly, physically broken? I use this term to describe when one's heart is not at peace to the point that it feels almost completely overburdened with pain and hurt. It is as if it does not function properly and must be fixed.

I would venture to say that when you state that you have a broken heart, it is because your spirit has not found peace in the remembrance of God. You have not been able to find a balance between the challenge you are having and the promise of God's mercy upon you. Given this state, you are giving your body permission to stay in a place of darkness and despair. You are allowing your negative thoughts to control your daily reactions to life.

Some die of a broken heart. They do not have the strength to battle all the tests that are being leveled upon them at that moment or over a period of time. What they don't realize though, or what they don't have the strength to consider, is the fact that Allah has the ability to reconcile your affairs if you let Him in. You don't have to go it alone. I understand that the pain of death, rejection, or some other loss can place you in a state of outrage, total despair, and even temporary insanity. However, when our focus returns to reflecting on the fact that everything happens for a reason and nothing is by accident, we can begin to use our spiritual strength for support.

If we say we trust in God's word, we will be tested with that belief. In the Quran in Surah Ankabut 29:2, there is a verse that says:

"Do the people think that they will be left to say, 'We believe' and they will not be tried?"

Being tested/tried is mentioned multiple times within the Quran. If you truly are a believer, the tests will come, sometimes one after the other without relief for a long period of time. Your job is to continue having strong faith no matter the circumstances and allow God to be the support for you.

Broken hearts can be repaired. Spirituality can be too. They both can be strengthened. The trick is you must trust and believe that God has your back the whole time.

Spirituality is your soul trying to connect to God no matter what your life is throwing at you. It is remembering where you come from "originally" without your bodily form and desiring to get back there with the least scratches and scrapes. In the end, you want to approach your Lord knowing that you tried your best to hold onto what He had in store for you. Never give up. You can make it.

Disclaimer: In no way is this section meant to minimize how tragedy is handled by individuals. It is meant to give reminders that God is always there for us. It is meant to encourage us to continually refresh our commitment to His word and His promises so that when tragedy does strike, we are better equipped to handle it. My heart goes out to all who are suffering from a broken heart or who are being given tests greater than any that I can imagine. It is not easy, and I pray that you make it through.

Chapter 10

Personal Stories and Observations

The following stories are comprised of situations I have observed, my living truth, and the living truths of four women brave enough to expose their hearts so that you can benefit. I have great respect for these four ladies. They didn't have to open themselves up to discuss their battles with anxiety, stress, and spirituality, but they did.

Our challenges and experiences are those of so many others. Please read them completely. Let others read them. It took a lot of strength and contemplation for them to be able to give these to you. I pray that by sharing these, you will find a way to reconcile with your own anxiety, stress, and spiritual struggles. I appreciate my contributors so much. Thank you.

The acts of someone who is anxious are many. If you are not an anxiety sufferer, you will never understand the pressure that a person places upon themselves to behave in a certain way or to avoid doing so. The sufferer, if they are high-functioning, will do their best to not expose their inner struggles to anyone outside of their closest circle. Sometimes, even those close to them will not understand the depth that it reaches.

Compensating for their feelings becomes the new, daily normal. He or she may tidy up spaces excessively or remove themselves from areas where many people are gathered. They may become agitated when they cannot control their environment or overreact to the point where they become annoying to others. I have witnessed all of these examples and probably more that I didn't know were fueled by anxiety. I only learned this information within the last few years as I began working on my own issues. It is amazing what looks "normal" until you realize that it's not.

Here are some instances that I can recall where I believe anxiety, stress, and lack of spiritual balance played a part.

Story 1

Being the "strongest" one in the family, the one who never cries or reacts to anything, seems like you have the power position over everyone. You are the one that everyone comes to when something is wrong or even when something is right. You are the one who is entrusted with the deepest, darkest secrets of the entire family and probably your friends as well. You are the one who never shows fear or worry even though the world seems to be crashing down on everyone around you, including yourself. But what others do not know, is that not being able to express your true inner self to others is extremely painful. This position - this state as being everyone's rock - can take its toll. It can be one of the loneliest power positions ever created.

I used to think that having the ability to not show emotion was one of the greatest blessings I had seen. I looked at people who were like this and wondered how in the world they keep it all together. I would look up to them and believe that that is what I needed to survive horrible times. I have actually been taught this directly and indirectly throughout my entire life and I can say that I was pretty good at it. I never thought it was a bad thing until I started observing others around me as I got older – others who had the same "amazing" trait!

There were some people that I knew who had not grown up with very much in their lives and had not grown up with the type of support from family that I had grown up with. They were extremely strong and self-sufficient. They were some of the best problem solvers that I had ever seen. I would venture to say that they were not living, but they were truly surviving day after day. I thought it amazing the way that they lived their lives. I saw greatness within them that if you blinked you would miss. They were incredible poets and business people. They had hearts that were so big, yet they expressed their feelings in ways that were not the most beneficial to themselves.

Their spirits absolutely moved me each time I would encounter them. Where others may have seen thugs without a desire to be anything greater, I saw artists and misguided protectors of a generation to come. I saw mountains that stood firmly yet would crumble at the very touch of a soul that actually gave a darn. I saw life in these young people when their surroundings promoted death every day. I was drawn to their fire and resolve despite what others may have thought about them. I felt kinship with their souls, though we may have appeared to be mismatched at first or even second sight. I will never forget that feeling. It stays with me to this day.

What I also learned, the more I paid attention and the closer we became, was that there was so much pain and disappointment brewing within them. It came out in their words, in their actions, and in their lack of wanting to acknowledge feelings that everyone knew were there. Their strength and dismissive attitudes masked a whole other world that most would never even see. If you were somehow able to catch a glimpse of it, your acknowledgments would be denied. That is the nature of the beast. You can never truly be open because open makes you vulnerable, and that vulnerability makes you seemingly weak. It is a never-ending cycle of pain. Might I also add, that these feelings and actions or reactions are passed down generation after generation if they are not dealt with at some point. It is not a great way to live but from my observations and conversations with them, those who live that life believe that it is one of the only and best ways to survive.

I have gone through phases like this. I have believed that others could use the prayers, or the blessings more than I could. I believed that by not expressing my true feelings on an issue, that I was saving myself from being disappointed with the outcome. I am now too old to believe that something like that is true. I now believe that strong spiritual connections can deter many of these unhealthy thoughts, feelings and actions. We just have to put in the work and ignore negative energy from others that may keep us from striving to be our best selves.

To be healthy, you must have a way to express yourself and relieve yourself of some of the stresses of life that are pressing down on your body. You must be able to reconcile the feelings that you have. You must be able to move forward in a manner that provides you and your children with the best life possible. Apparent strength all the time is not without its consequences. If you do not feel the toll that it is taking on you today, you will feel it tomorrow or eventually. You must act now to prevent harm to you and your family. Find your spiritual sweet spot and let it work for you.

Quick Lesson

You are worthy of receiving the encouragement and support of others no matter who you are. You are worthy of achieving great things within your life no matter who you are. You are the one who holds the gifts that God gave you. No one can take them from you. Though some may try to make you feel less than worthy, you must mentally challenge those ideas and dismiss them as quickly as you are able. Do not let them settle within your heart and soul. It is hard to remove negativity that you have allowed to live within your body for years. It is much easier for negative people to remove themselves from your life once you decide that you are worth God's attention and mercy.

Story 2

In junior high school, I had a friend who talked a mile a minute and joked constantly. It was like there was no off button on her. I thought she was HILARIOUS! We got along quite well and remained friends throughout the three years. I believe we only stopped being close when she moved.

While in school though, I can remember her making bad choices as far as boys were concerned. She would choose a boy who had no interest in her and pursue him relentlessly. I know. It sounds like something that would normally happen in schools, right? Point taken. The boy was lukewarm in response and when he did engage her, he didn't treat her well. To my knowledge, he didn't hit her. He was just rude and dismissive with no regard for her feelings. Again, I get it and point taken.

My friend would laugh uncomfortably when talking about him, but I could see the pain in her eyes. She still wouldn't give up though. It was like she needed someone – anyone – to fill a void. To be completely rejected by this boy was not going to happen in her world. She did her best to control the situation. She carried on pretending that everything was fine. I carried on trying to support her, but I was dying on the inside at the toll it was taking on her. How, as a friend and at that age – an age that situations such as this should be handled by adults – could I leave her to fend for herself? I couldn't. I met her mother and I could see that the relationship between them was quite strained. Maybe this is where my friend's desire for acceptance at any cost came from.

She taught me lessons that I would carry with me for life but only utilize when I was older:

- Know when to stop pursuing people whether it be a romantic relationship, friendship, or business relationship.
- The perception of being ok may not always work in my favor long-term, but it may possibly work short-term. This should not be the default for my life though.
- Sometimes it's best to move on.

Story 3

There was a young lady who was actually similar to the one in story 2. I wasn't close friends with her though. I met her through mutual friends of ours. I was in my teens at the time and we were hanging out at a friend's house. This girl, who was younger than me, had a boyfriend. I knew him, but I had no idea that he was capable of the behavior that I witnessed.

As my friends and I sat and talked in one room, the young lady, her boyfriend, and a few others sat in another room talking. A few minutes later they both came walking around the corner. At first, I thought they were playing around, but then I changed my mind. She was nervously laughing as he was belittling her. He even slapped her and she continued laughing and crying (*from laughter* of course).

As a teen, I didn't know what to do. I had never seen a situation like this before. Those who knew them better appeared to have given up reacting because the girl stayed with her boyfriend no matter what. I was shocked! I knew this wasn't right, but I had no power to stop it. I wondered how a girl could stay with someone who treated her like that.

I learned later that she didn't really deal with her family much and she didn't want to be cast out by the whole group. If she said anything, that would mean the possibility of being alone. I suppose that anxiety outweighed protecting her own life. Sadly, years later I also learned that situations like this occur between adults. May we all be protected from the evil and dysfunction of others and that which lies within ourselves.

Lessons learned:

- Never stay in a dangerous situation for the sake of loneliness. It's my life. I will preserve it.
- Make sure my daughter knows that she is loved.
- Make sure my sons know to respect and protect women.
- Make sure my daughter and sons all know what healthy relationships and healthy problem solving looks like.

Story 4

A professional that I knew spoke of her fear of public speaking. It was amazing to me because she has a very people-oriented profession (which I will keep to myself). She speaks to people daily and appears to be so calm; however, she told me that she gets upset stomach and worse when asked to speak in front of a group.

I know in the past that I had heard movie stars say that this happened to them as well. How can a movie star have anxiety and still perform? I guess growing up, I did it too, and I continue to thrive to this day despite the fact. Personally knowing that someone you trust has a condition that you have suffered from for many years is somehow comforting. I found a kinship and a peace with that knowledge, even with all of the chaos going on in my mind.

More wonderful lessons learned:

- Carry on and succeed despite your mind and body trying to hold you back.
- I am not alone.

Gail Fripp's Story

It was a regular day - regular as in I was in my usual state of worrying about things that I could not control. I would worry about friends. I would worry about family members. I would worry about my own well-being. I thought that while I was anxiously worrying, it was normal to feel chest pains and body aches. I carried on and just went about my day.

Well, this particular day they were extremely painful. I had been concerned about multiple things and was unable to control my thoughts regarding them. I knew that my chest was hurting, but I felt if I just relaxed a little while or went to sleep that it would go away. That was not the case.

I woke up in the middle of the night feeling as if I was having a heart attack. I sat up in my bed with a pain that felt like someone had struck me in the chest and was twisting their fist right and left through my body. I had a pain in my back that was sharp and opposite the pain in my chest. My breathing was stifled and I couldn't take a full breath. I thought of going to the living room to lay down so I wouldn't disturb my husband. Then I thought to myself: "What happens if I am having a heart attack and can't make it back to the room. Will my children find me there?" I couldn't bear to do that, so I stayed in my room. Some time went by and the pain did not stop.

It was around 3 in the morning or so. I woke my husband up to let him know what was happening. He asked if I wanted to go to the hospital and I said I'd wait a little longer. Needless to say, shortly after that, I gave in and went to the hospital. That was one of the worst days that I have ever had. The thought in my mind that I may not see my children again. I thought of all the things that were unfinished. I thought of all the things that I wanted to do and say that I had not done and said. Being a homeschool mom, I even thought of the lesson plans that were not finished so that somebody else could teach the kids in my absence. It might be funny now, but I was a crying wreck!

So, we get to the hospital and run through all of the tests. I even shared a room with someone that I didn't know. That sucked. At the end of it all, after they found nothing seriously wrong with me, after the doctor gave me a muscle relaxer because he felt it was a muscle strain, after I fought my germophobic tendencies to save my life, I went home. The diagnosis (my personal diagnosis): I was a freaking anxious, stressed out sister who almost killed myself worrying about things that were out of my control. Yep. Sad but true. I allowed my thoughts to control me in a way that was not beneficial to me or those around me. I unknowingly chose to allow negativity to dictate my next actions. I allowed myself to believe that if I worried enough for others, that they would, in turn, worry for themselves and fix their own issues. I was wrong. This was not a sustainable way for me to live and it affected me and my household.

From that day to the current day, I have vowed to never allow that to happen to me again. By the will of God, I will never allow myself to be in such a state of mind that my life is put in peril. My children and my husband need me to be at my best. I need me to be at my best.

This mindset change has helped me put many of my thoughts and actions into perspective and has allowed me to speak out on the dangers of holding on to anxiety and stress like they are your best friends. I feel spreading this message is one of the major things that I was sent here to do. I feel that I am here to encourage others to allow themselves to be supported even when they feel it's unnecessary or when they feel themselves unworthy. By the way, I am still perfecting it. It's not a race and I am now fine with that. One day and one step at a time, with God's guidance, I will carry on and be much better than the day before.

Jennifer Villa's Story

I used to stress myself all the time - enough to take medication. I have finally found many somethings as of late to help relieve that stress and the strains it causes. People used to feel my crazy energy. They didn't know how to take me. Well things had to change after so many years of insanity and pain not only for me, but my husband.

Life was becoming unbearable. I started yoga but didn't get it at first. I learned to just breathe. Then it clicked. I dove in head first. My life has changed so much. I have become less dependent on medication. My belief is that with continued work with practicing meditation, I can make it through these issues by changing the way I look and think about my life.

I defuse oil at night, candles during yoga at night with some meditation crystals, etc. I feel the difference and so do all those around me. I feel it is the way of life I am supposed to live. I am on the right path. I know how this may sound to some, but I want to help people even if it means putting it all out there. This is the real me. Take me or not.

Shareefa Siri M. Carrion's Story

How Anxiety Has Touched My Life

As a former single parent, anxiety and stress were part of my life. I did not realize they were part of my life, nor did I know "THEY" had a name. However, I knew how they felt. Anxiety and stress feels like something in me has died, over and over again.

There is one particular situation that stays with me. I was young and newly married living in Amarillo, TX of all places. We had a little girl and I was pregnant again. Just like many marriages, we were going through some hardships that involved drinking, an extramarital affair, and unemployment. But the hardest thing for me was being married to someone who was not practicing their deen (religion). It was important for me to raise our kids in an Islamic household. This was something that we discussed before marriage and now, during our marriage, none of the things we discussed was happening.

I finally got to a point where I had to make some serious decisions. Do I continue to raise children in an un-Islamic household or do I leave and become a single mom? I finally realized I was so stressed and filled with anxiety. All I could do was cry and sleep. I did not know what to do, where to go, or how I was going to raise children by myself. All I kept remembering was that I did not want to be a single mom like my mom. I wanted the married life – a two parent household, raising our children together.

I finally came to a point where I could not handle any more of the ill behavior from my now ex-husband. I asked him to leave. Soon after I found out I was pregnant with twins.

I remember the day I found out I was pregnant with twins. I was in the hospital room with a coworker. She was in active labor and I was teasing her about breathing and pushing the baby out. As I left her room, to go to my doctor's appointment, she yells, "I hope you have twins!"

I arrive to the doctor's office and the doctor is performing a sonogram to check the "baby". As he is performing the sonogram, he tells me, "Well kid, I have good news. I have head A and head B." My first thought was, my baby has two heads?" He then proceeds to tell me I am having twins! Yes Twins! Right then and there everything came to a head. I fell out crying, right there in the doctor's office. It wasn't a tear drop crying, it was a full on sob with snot running down my face type of crying. When I looked up the doctor was looking at me like what is going on? All he kept saying was, "It's ok kid! I had a mom in here smaller than you that pushed out twins!" That's when I told him I was divorcing my husband.

At that time, I was 18 weeks pregnant. Before that, I spent my time working, raising my daughter, and dealing with an alcoholic husband. When I wasn't working, I was trying to figure out what to do with my life and my daughter's life. There were times I was able to calm my nerves and emotions. However, when I started to think, my anxiety and stress levels increased. For the first 2 trimesters I was in denial - denial of my pregnancy, denial of my husband and his behavior, denial that I was going to divorce him and raise my children alone. It was easier to deal with my anxiety and stress if I just denied everything, even though I felt my world falling apart.

Finally, during the 3rd trimester, I gave in to my anxiety and stress and I let go. I let go of the anxiety and fear. I spent a lot of my time praying and asking Allah (God) for the strength to get through this hard time. When I did that, when I let go, it seemed like all my anxiety and stress melted away. I could sleep at night. I could eat and I was actually smiling right up to the point when my water broke. Then, the anxiety, fear, and stress came flooding back. The dam broke when I had to call my best friend to come get me and take me to the hospital because my then husband was nowhere to be found. None of my family was there to be with me in the delivery room. I tried to hold on to my serenity and peace, but as each minute passed by, my peace and serenity were being peeled away like an onion.

After I had the babies, I was home again and alone. Thinking about everything under the stars and praying, asking Allah (God) for a sign as to what I needed to do. I was learning to leave my affairs in the hands of Allah (God). I know that now. However, at that time, I didn't know that. My anxiety and stress seemed as though it was worse than before. I could not focus on anything in front of me. I was always thinking of the past and the things I should have done, or I was thinking of the future and the things I need to do.

During this difficult time of my life, so many things happened. I had lost my job and one of my twins, twin B, was born premature and had pneumonia. Rent was due, we had no food, and I was dealing with postpartum depression. There was just so much going on. I could not continue to juggle everything that was happening. At that time, I was focusing on my prayers and keeping my mind in a state of positive thinking. After a while I just didn't know what else to do but surrender to Allah (God). I did not have a job, so I spent my day praying to Allah for relief.

I remember spreading my rug out in the living room and setting my Quran on the wooden stand next to my prayer rug. When I was not crying I was praying to Allah and reading Quran. When I just couldn't pray any more nor read, I tried to get some sleep and take care of my babies. When I sat to pray and read, I felt my anxiety and stress melting away. There were a few ayats (verses) that stayed with me - ones that reminded me that Allah is with those who are patient. My absolute favorite ayah from the Quran is, "With every hardship comes ease." (94:6) Even now this small verse gives me comfort.

Once I read these verses and BELIEVED IN THEM, I knew I would be ok. I knew Allah had my back. I knew Allah would not place on me anything more than I can bear.

Like I said, I had no job and no money. I barely had gas to get around. Alhamdulillah, Allah provided for me. I opened my freezer, there was food there. My children had milk. When rent was due Allah, opened the way for me to get the rent paid.

When I look back on this difficult part of my life, I sometimes cry. But most of the time I sit back and smile and think. Only Allah got me through this hardship.

I am thankful for this experience from Allah. It was because of this experience I learned about Allah and how to relieve my anxiety and stress.

N's Story

The person that the world around me has grown accustomed to seeing and interacting with is the person that I am when I need to be someone. It's the character that I've created when I'm too insecure to be the one that I naturally am. It's the little girl who had unmet needs and learned how to do things for herself. It's the little girl who recognizes when other people have unmet needs and tries her hardest to do things for them.

I grew up in a large family. The child of entrepreneurs, our life was anything but typical. There were many days that we were at work late with our parents, and many others when work came home. Although most wouldn't believe it now, I was something of a shy child and didn't like to make a whole lot of noise. If there was something that I wanted or needed, there was a good chance that I wasn't going to be very vocal about it because I feared the rejection of being told 'no.' Even worse, I feared being told 'yes' and then never getting what I'd asked for.

I started to do things for myself. Although this was prompted by a desire to meet my needs, it was seen by others as being a self-starter and a sign of maturity and independence. When I was seen doing things for myself, it was interpreted as a sign that I no longer needed things done for me. It's interesting because I never really wanted to do most of what I did. But I did it so that it would get done. And on a certain level, I began to resent those around me who I believed should have been responsible for meeting my needs.

As I grew older, it became apparent to those around me that I could take care of myself. And it had long become my mindset that if I didn't take care of myself, I wouldn't be taken care of. Don't get me wrong, I didn't have to get a job in the 3rd grade to keep the lights on, but sometimes I had to prepare my own meals, do my own laundry, and so forth. The biggest area that I felt neglected was emotionally. Resentment and emotional neglect do not make for a happy, healthy individual. They are, however, the perfect ingredients for stress. And stressed I was.

Although I was stressed, I was what most people would consider a strong person. I am tall (for a woman). I am educated and well-spoken. I have southern manners without the southern drawl and for as long as I can remember, people have felt comfortable coming to me with their problems. I have spent a good portion of my life helping those who could not, or would not, help themselves. I used to wonder why so many people came to me with their issues and then, it dawned on me - it was because I was strong. What none of them knew was that what they perceived as strength was nothing more than my desire to not be neglected. It was an attempt to be whole, to be taken care of and what I thought was normal. I was constantly in "helper" mode and almost never took any time to reflect and realize the damage I was a party to.

As time passed, I became increasingly closed off emotionally. As I became more emotionally fragile, I developed a mean outer shell. In other words, I started being mean to people. I wasn't excessive about it. I didn't go around bullying anyone. But I had a smart mouth, which became a loud mouth, and eventually a smart, loud mouth. This persona was very uncomfortable for me to keep up as it was contrary to my natural inclinations, but once I got it going, I became afraid to let it go. Instead of being a better person, to offset all the unpleasantness I increased the number of people I helped whether it was through tutoring or bringing someone snacks to school.

While I really enjoyed helping people, I typically did this not only at my own expense but often to my own detriment. I felt needed and used at the same time. When I was busy helping someone, I didn't feel as stressed as I did when I had down time. But I all but stopped taking care of myself. I took from what little I had with little to no replenishment. I was trying to pour from an empty cup.

By the time I got to high school, my health began to wane. I went from being a healthy young person to having a severe and inexplicable case of acid reflux and losing way too much weight. I was on ulcer medication by 16 and weighed just around 130 pounds when the ideal weight for my height and frame was much closer to 145 pounds. I developed a tumor in my lymph nodes. I slept 12-14 hours a day. When I ate, it was processed and most likely covered in chocolate.

In the process of trying to fill my needs and provide sometimes unsolicited assistance to those around me, I had figured out how to stay busy! I never had a spare moment. No time to rest. Never enough sleep. Meals hardly ever hot from the stove. Thrifting clothes because I liked both the style and the price. Always all over the place. Never a moment to slow, to stop, and realize that the incessant need to move was fueled in large part by the fact that I no longer knew how to be alone with myself. If I were alone, I would have to face me, all of me, and all the insecurities of that unfulfilled little girl. If I slowed down, I would may be met with the almost crippling anxiety and discomfort of having learned the truth about my fragility but not having the courage to be that truth.

If I were moving and attending to the crises of others, I wouldn't have to slow down and recognize the crisis within. I wouldn't have to recognize that I was not actually hungry. I didn't notice that my assistance wasn't requested. I could keep chugging along, ignoring my weight issues, reflux, and general mediocre health that had developed due to my unmanaged stress and I could blame all the extra pounds on my little ones. If I stayed busy, I didn't have to answer any questions about myself.

But it happened. That quiet, alone space that I deathly avoided - it came, all at once. I don't know how or when, but I know that it closed in on me and I was bare, exposed, and lonely. I was in rooms full of familiar faces, but I felt like a stranger. I was presented with the character I was portraying, and I immediately knew that she and I were not the same. I'd allowed a lifetime of stress to determine the trajectory of my public persona while hiding a perfectly good, perfectly stable person behind the hoopla.

There I stood, in my truth. All the excuses to maintain a subpar version of a fictitious person came tumbling down and I was struck by the deception of it all. I was upset with people for not knowing a version of me that I'd never shown them. I was upset with them for not allowing me to exist comfortably in a space that allows my reality. And I realized that it was all on me.

While there may have been a time when I was unable to verbalize my wants and needs, that time had passed. I was an adult and fully capable of expressing myself when it came to any other matter. So, I became confronted with the reality that no one was holding onto that stress except for me. I clung to it. Clenched it for dear life, as it had become a part of who I thought I had to be. But once I decided that I was ready to step into the truth I'd previously realized, I knew that it was my responsibility alone to address anything I was dragging around from my childhood. I had to confront it, deal with it, and move on. So, I did.

I began talking to God. I don't mean in a prayerful manner. I mean straight up, conversation-style talking. Initially I thought I was going to talk to myself, but I quickly realized that He was much better equipped to handle any and everything. I talked, and I talked, and I talked some more. Sometimes I cried. Sometimes I couldn't even verbalize the thoughts, but I knew He could still hear them.

At times, I reflected on past experiences that felt particularly damaging and attempted to dissect them from multiple points of view and to ascertain why they still evoked so much emotion from me after so much time. Other times I spoke of the future, what I could accomplish, what I would accomplish, and what my accomplishments would mean for my offspring. Sometimes I would go over the many things I had on my many to-do lists. Other times I would talk about a specific person, the nature of my relationship with them and what I could possibly do to improve it.

Talking to God is unlike talking to anyone else. Although you don't hear an actual response in words, He responds in all sorts of ways. Once I was open to His responses, I saw Him in places that were previously desolate and barren. I saw Him in ways I'd never seen Him before. Once I took myself to God, open and honest, I began seeing Him. It was amazing.

I occasionally shared my "conversations" with those I trusted and loved but often kept my talks private. I find that when I feel the world closing in on me I've almost always allowed too much time to pass without talking to God. Some call it meditation. Some think of it as prayer. For me, it felt like talking because I talked to Him as if He were right there with me and we were the best of friends. And He, in true form, responded as such.

Sonya Rodgers' Story

The past 4 years I've been on a major "personal growth spurt". I didn't intend on it, it just sort of happened because of life events. I started homeschooling and started my own business all at the same time. When you are done reading my story, I hope you are encouraged by how I've found peace in my purpose and I hope that you find your own!

Several years ago, I was introduced to something that rocked my world! It helped my family so much that I decided to share with others and turn it into my business. I couldn't keep something so amazing to myself and I knew I had something that so many people needed. Now if you know me, you know that I hate MLM (Multi-Level Marketing), and I hate selling ANYTHING. On top of that, I'm an introvert! So, starting my own business was very hard for me, but my team grew quickly! So quickly in fact that, unknowingly, it took my focus off helping people and turned it to wanting to make more money.

A couple of years ago, I really started struggling with thoughts like "I'm not good enough" or "I can't do anything right." I felt that if I couldn't make my personal goals as a mom, teacher, or business owner that I just wasn't good enough! In hindsight, I wouldn't say I was depressed, but I definitely was not happy or content with anything. I was worrying about everything, not sleeping, angry all the time, and it was spewing into every area of my life.

My husband kept reminding me to talk to God, to lean on Him, to ask Him to guide me. I would just nod in agreement and do nothing about it. After some time, I kept feeling a tug in my heart that this wasn't me and it wasn't what God wanted for me. So I started talking to Him more, praying more, and spending more time with Him.

One day I was throwing a fit about things not going my way and not reaching one of my goals because we knew if we were going to keep our girls at the university model school they attended, we would need an extra income. So, I was really upset because I knew my kids were in the program they were supposed to be in. I also felt that God had led me to this business as a way to provide financially for us to keep sending the girls there!

In the middle of my tantrum my husband looked me in the eye and said, "Oh, so you're upset that you didn't reach the rank you wanted? I understand...but just answer this one question...didn't you start this business because you wanted to help people?" Those words pierced my heart.

I went for months afterward asking and praying to God to bring me joy and peace in any situation, and an amazing thing happened. I started hearing stories from people about how I had helped them. I started meeting people on my team that I had never met before and hearing their amazing stories. I started making new friendships that led me closer to God! And if that weren't enough, I got a job at my kids' school working only 2 days a week - the 2 days they go to school, so I don't work on our 3 homeschool days. That gave us an amazing discount at their school.

So now, to keep my focus on helping others (and off me, me, me), I go back to notes people have written me. I keep scripture up all over our house, and I look into my mirror and speak life into my situation because I know that God has a plan and purpose for me! Keeping my focus on Him and on helping others reminds me of what is most important in life!

It's hard to put into words the emotion and all the ups and downs I went through. Just reading this, it probably doesn't sound like much, but if you knew the amount of personal growth I've had the past 4 years, you would be amazed! I'm learning things, doing things, seeing things, and trying things that I never have before! It's scary and it's hard, but God has given me a mission and I know I can't back down. Being a homeschool mom and a business owner were 2 things I said I wouldn't do, and it's amazing the growth I've experienced by doing something I was afraid to do!

Reflections

I wanted to add a small section with touches of wisdom, power, and love. These small pieces of light are meant to spark meaningful conversations and personal growth and to show you one of the ways that I reduce my anxiety and stress – by liberating the stored energy with words.

When I write, I am releasing my soul onto the pages. I use words to help my readers grasp the intricate labyrinth that is my mind as it takes you on an endless journey through this life and worlds beyond. When I write, I desire to pull you into my space – to let you see what I see – to help you see what you are missing if you only knew.

When I write, I teach yet I learn. I teach what I know, and I learn that my limits are nowhere in sight. When I write, I look for the lessons that the reader can give me as they respond to my musings – lessons that I take and pass on to those who will benefit from them. When I write I shine from the inside out and hope to light a path for you.

It is my hope that you analyze, connect to, and internalize the following passages and see how they apply to you and your life. I want you to perceive your situation from a different angle. I pray that this section helps someone even in a small way.

J.W.C – Judging While Connected

Women may be different on the outside, but we are all fighting for something similar. We want to teach our kids the best lessons. We want to be a wonderful companion for a spouse. We want to accomplish the things that we desire. We want to look at ourselves and be happy with what we see. Just thinking about this connection between us breaks down so many barriers if you only sit and think about it. The woman that you look at with such disdain and horror may want the same thing you want but may be taking a different path to try to get there. Don't be so quick to judge. We are all closer than you think.

Who Did You Meet Today?

As spiritual beings, when we meet someone we sometimes feel that we already know them or that we should avoid them as much as possible. We feel that they are naturally and genuinely our friend or our sister -or not. We are guided to this person through no effort of our own. If we stop and see the beauty of that act, we would begin to look at every interaction with our sister as something incredibly amazing. We may be guided to be the catalyst for her next rising, or we may be placed as a barrier to her push forward. I like to say that we can always learn something from those we meet whether it be good or bad. There is always a lesson. Whether we see the lesson and actually use it is another story. So, who did you meet today and what lesson did you learn?

True Faith

For those who have not the foresight, true faith in something unseen may sound like a complete waste of time. They may believe if it cannot be physically proven, it doesn't exist. For many others, this belief in something greater, something more powerful than all of us is, is exactly what is needed to maintain balance on a daily basis. We live for true faith and we die on true faith.

This quiet spiritual element is a driving force in my life and the lives of my family members. I don't see any other explanation for me waking up another day and the next person passing away, sometimes suddenly. How do we breathe without any prompting of our own? How do we explain the development cycle of babies? How do we explain the complete sense of peace after tragedy has stricken us? More obviously, how do we explain what we naturally see – the giving of rain, the sustaining of trees, the variety of animal life which no human had a hand in creating. All of it came from somewhere. True Faith. We didn't get here on our own. We don't survive on our own.

The Beauty of Life

Life is beautiful for so many reasons: the friends you make, the family you have, the green grass and tall trees, and on and on. It can also be beautiful because of the internal peace that you achieve.

This peace feels like God personally took your hand and walked you through your trials and tribulations while laying you down softly after each one. It feels like a soothing massage that gives you goosebumps with every stroke. It feels like soft whispers that reinforce your strength when you start feeling doubt. It feels like...like...the real you when you are not worried about acceptance from others because you completely accept yourself. That is true peace – true freedom.

If You Leave Me As I Am

If you leave me as I am, I will grow strong.

I will absorb the world and use it to my advantage.

I will advance as the seasons advance – different with each revolution, yet with a familiar presence.

But if you try to contain my spirit, I will rebel – not on purpose, but because it is my nature to flourish.

I will be reduced to battling my passion to move forward and your resistance to my rise.

Is that what you want for me? I think not.

So leave me and love me as I am. I will reciprocate the gesture.

I am only as God made me and I have accepted my earthly role.

Will you also accept it and allow me to grow?

Faith and Action

God has promised that if we have true faith in Him and do good deeds that we will be rewarded.

"Whoever does righteousness, whether male or female, while he is a believer - We will surely cause him to live a good life, and We will surely give them their reward [in the Hereafter] according to the best of what they used to do."   **Quran 16:97**

That requires trusting in what we cannot see and believing, with all that we have, that He will deliver on His word. Professing our faith rolls off our tongues like water, but are we telling ourselves the truth? That is why it is so important that we involve ourselves in the active search for a strong connection to Him.

Nothing happens in this life without action – not even faith. Do all that you can to guard against what will cause your faith to decrease. Ask for clarity on what your path is and ask for strength as you travel upon it. Be open to what you will not see coming but what will surely test you. If you breathe, you are still in the service of the Most High and are capable of improving your state. Don't waste your opportunities to be greater than you are right now.

The Fight

Do you only follow what you can see?

Have you not learned the taste of true faith within what is hidden?

Maybe you are sitting on the fence – saying you believe yet stressing daily.

This is not faith. This is insanity and lies to yourself.

God knows what you reveal and what you conceal, so you cannot lie to Him.

Don't distress. Choose to do better and act on it.

Check yourself where you stand, sit, and lie.

Arrogance has no place in the fight for the liberation of your soul.

Conclusion

I want to thank you all for desiring to make beautiful changes in your lives. I've been there, and I want to prevent as many people as possible from struggling and not knowing where to turn, like I did. With this book, I hope that I gave you a glimpse into the world of anxiety, stress, and spiritual balance – a world that may look similar to your own or someone you know. I hope you now know that you are not alone. I pray that I have encouraged you to keep going if you have begun to help yourself surpass these challenges. If not, I pray that you have the strength to begin to do so today.

This was just an introduction and a catalyst to get you moving towards a more peaceful life for you. Each of these subjects would need a separate book to attempt to do them justice. Please purchase a copy or two and give them away if you believe that the lessons contained within will help others in any way. Don't keep the knowledge to yourself.

I speak because someone spoke to me and for me. I heard a brother named Trevor Otts, one of the founders of an amazing organization called Black CEO (Che Brown is the other founder) state: "Don't let a door that was opened for you close for someone else." Will you? I'm cheering for you all!

Lovingly and positively,

Gail Fripp

Resources

Gail Fripp

Follow me on Facebook: @gailfripp3R

Follow me on Instagram and Twitter: @gailfripp

Website: http://gailfripp.com

Email: gail@gailfripp.com

To get on my mailing list, go to: bit.ly/survive3r

Hasan and Naa'ila Clay

They are fabulous certified counselors in Atlanta, but their practice is global. They counsel singles, couples, anxiety sufferers, and so many more by various means. Contact them at:

http://hasanandnaaila.com/

Anxiety and Depression Association of America

This website holds a wealth of information but should not be your only source of diagnosing yourself or treating yourself. Get further help from a certified counselor or physician when necessary.

http://adaa.org

About the Author

Gail Fripp is a Muslim, wife, homeschooling mother of six, entrepreneur, author, artist, perpetual student of life and persistent seeker of personal peace. She grew up Christian and her family is majority Christian. She has always been passionate about living life on her own terms and helping others do the same. She has done this in the past by creating and running a girls' youth group, speaking at conferences, being a Girl Scout leader for almost 5 years, speaking on panels, and running websites focused on women, to name a few. Currently, she finds joy in reaching a greater audience by utilizing live video discussions and interviews.

She holds a bachelor's degree in business and was pursuing a master's degree in Islamic studies before shifting her focus back to homeschool and family matters. (Family first. Always.) Gail has been married for more than 20 years and is still learning and adjusting to life's natural changes. It's part of the process and she accepts the beautiful challenge. She believes in strong marriages making strong families. None of that happens without knowing yourself and being confident that you are blessed with the power and ability to design and accomplish your vision.

Why She Does What She Does

Her interest in the areas of anxiety, stress, and spiritual balance began when she realized that from a young age, she hesitated to be confident and to excel in her own natural gifts. It held her back in life. She noticed the same traits in many women and girls she encountered over more than three decades. Gail knew she needed to begin changing her mindset and speaking out so that others could gain strength from her experiences and newly acquired knowledge.

The Goal

Her goal is now to make a targeted effort to develop that self-confidence in women and girls to the point that they thrive in friendships, as spouses and parents, in business, and in spirit.

www.ingramcontent.com/pod-product-compliance
Lightning Source LLC
Chambersburg PA
CBHW071156090426
42736CB00012B/2349